CYBER THREATS

# DENIAL-OF-SERVICE ATTACKS

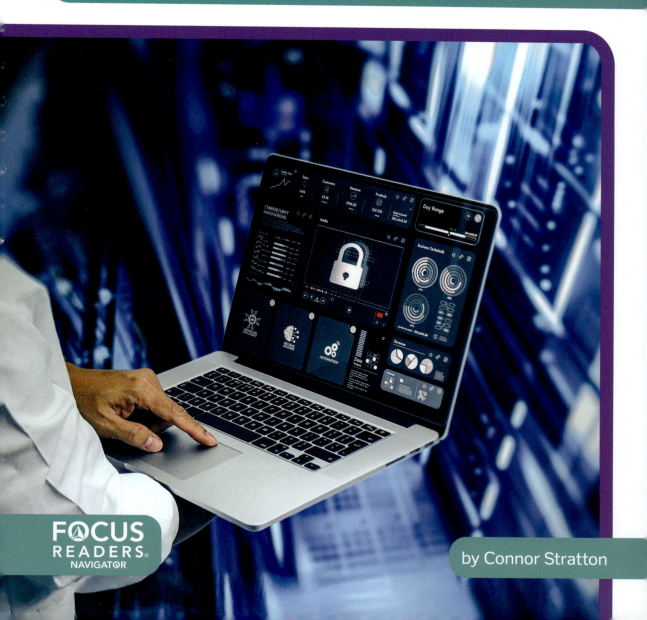

by Connor Stratton

## WWW.FOCUSREADERS.COM

Copyright © 2026 by Focus Readers®, Mendota Heights, MN 55120. All rights reserved. No part of this book may be reproduced or utilized in any form or by any means without written permission from the publisher.

Focus Readers is distributed by North Star Editions:
sales@northstareditions.com | 888-417-0195

Produced for Focus Readers by Red Line Editorial.

Photographs ©: iStockphoto, cover, 1; Shutterstock Images, 4–5, 7, 8–9, 11, 14–15, 17, 19, 20–21, 23, 25, 27, 29; Red Line Editorial, 13

**Library of Congress Cataloging-in-Publication Data**
Names: Stratton, Connor, author
Title: Denial-of-service attacks / by Connor Stratton.
Description: Mendota Heights, MN: Focus Readers, [2026] | Series: Cyber threats | Includes index. | Audience term: juvenile | Audience: Grades 4-6 Focus Readers
Identifiers: LCCN 2024059384 (print) | LCCN 2024059385 (ebook) | ISBN 9798889985167 hardcover | ISBN 9798889985778 pdf | ISBN 9798889985488 ebook
Subjects: LCSH: Denial of service attacks--Juvenile literature
Classification: LCC HV6773.15.C97 S77 2026 (print) | LCC HV6773.15.C97 (ebook) | DDC 364.16/8--dc23/eng/20250211
LC record available at https://lccn.loc.gov/2024059384
LC ebook record available at https://lccn.loc.gov/2024059385

Printed in the United States of America
Mankato, MN
082025

## ABOUT THE AUTHOR
Connor Stratton writes and edits nonfiction children's books. He lives in Minnesota.

# TABLE OF CONTENTS

**CHAPTER 1**
## Cyberattacks in Ukraine  5

**CHAPTER 2**
## How DoS Attacks Work  9

**CHAPTER 3**
## Purpose and Impact  15

**CHAPTER 4**
## Fighting DDoS Attacks  21

**CYBER SAFETY**
## Avoiding DDoS Attacks  28

Focus Questions • 30
Glossary • 31
To Learn More • 32
Index • 32

**CHAPTER 1**

# CYBERATTACKS IN UKRAINE

On February 15, 2022, Russian **hackers** carried out an attack. They targeted key Ukrainian websites. They hit banking, government, and military sites. Hackers flooded the sites with fake **traffic**. The sites couldn't handle it. They shut down for hours. This is known as a distributed denial-of-service (DDoS) attack.

The 2022 attack was the largest DDoS attack to ever hit Ukraine.

Ukrainians also started getting fake bank messages. People felt confused and worried. On February 23, Russian hackers launched another DDoS attack. Ukrainian government sites went down again.

The next day, Russia invaded Ukraine. A brutal war followed. Armies shot at one another in the streets. They fired weapons at cities. Tens of thousands of people died.

Meanwhile, cyberattacks raged online. Hackers on both sides carried them out. DDoS attacks were the most common. They interrupted communication. They created panic. They also made other hacks easier. Hackers were able to steal

The Russia-Ukraine War included many physical attacks. Russia targeted major cities such as Kyiv.

data. They spied on enemies. They even attacked important **infrastructure**.

Cyber threats had existed for years. But their role increased in the Russia-Ukraine War. This change alarmed many computer experts. Cyberattacks seemed more dangerous than ever.

**CHAPTER 2**

# HOW DoS ATTACKS WORK

The internet is home to massive amounts of information. This information is stored on computers called servers. Often, many servers are connected to one another. Groups of connected computers are known as networks.

Computer servers are often stored in big buildings. These buildings are called data centers.

These server networks power the internet. Suppose someone wants to look at a website. She taps a link on her tablet. The tap sends her request to a server. The server has stored the most recent version of the website. It sends the website to the person's tablet. Now she can view the site.

This process takes energy and data. A single person does not use much of either. But often, many users visit the same site at the same time. The site experiences high traffic. When that happens, the network needs much more energy and data to keep working. Servers cannot always handle the extra traffic.

Each piece of information that a computer sends is called a packet.

Sometimes extra traffic happens by accident. A site might suddenly become very popular. People around the world try to access it. The flood of traffic stops the site from working. However, a hacker may try to crash a network on purpose. He uses his computer to flood the target network. That may cause the network to stop working. This is called a denial-of-service (DoS) attack.

A distributed denial-of-service (DDoS) attack is more powerful. This attack uses more than one computer. Often, hackers break into other people's computers. They use **malware** to do this. A group of hacked computers is called a botnet. Botnets can

## RENTING A BOTNET

Most people do not have the skill to be hackers. They cannot carry out a DDoS attack themselves. However, some hackers rent out botnets. Anyone can pay money to use the hackers' botnets. That lets more people plan DDoS attacks. In fact, kids as young as nine years old have hired botnets. Some took down their schools' networks.

flood networks with much more traffic. So, they can take down much stronger networks. Botnets also make it difficult to know who carried out a DDoS attack.

## HOW BOTNETS WORK

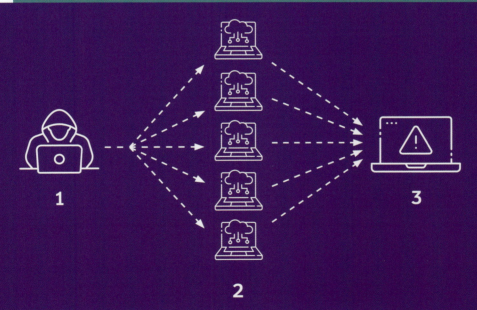

1. A hacker sends a command from a botnet server.
2. The command takes over many computers.
3. The botnet attacks the victim's server.

CHAPTER 3

# PURPOSE AND IMPACT

Hackers use DoS and DDoS attacks for many reasons. One purpose is to protest. A hacker may oppose the actions of a company or government. So, the hacker uses DDoS attacks on the group's website. Then, people cannot use that site. The disruption also brings attention. Sometimes the company or government

Some hackers compare DDoS protests to sit-ins. Both actions can bring attention or change.

15

feels pressure. It may change its actions after the attack.

DDoS attacks often happen in online gaming, too. Sometimes gamers feel angry after they lose. They may carry out DDoS attacks on the game's servers. Then no one can play the game.

Other gamers want to gain an edge. They use DDoS attacks against their opponents. They flood other **consoles** or computers with traffic. Other players experience **lag** or get disconnected. After that, it's easier for the hackers to win.

Money is another common reason for DDoS attacks. Hackers may target a company or government. They take down

DDoS attacks are common in multiplayer role-playing and action games.

its servers with DDoS attacks. Then they demand a **ransom**. They say they'll stop the attack for a price. These types of attacks can cost millions of dollars. They can also change how a group is seen. For example, a bank may appear less dependable after an attack.

Hackers also use DDoS attacks to distract people from other cybercrimes. For instance, hackers may want to steal data or spy. So, they start a DDoS attack. Stopping the attack takes a lot of focus. As a result, the hackers' other actions might not be noticed.

## 398 MILLION A SECOND

In 2023, Google faced a record-setting DDoS attack. The attack lasted just minutes. But at one point, the company's servers received 398 million requests each second. That year, approximately 335 million people lived in the United States. Suppose every person in the country visited the same website at the same time. The traffic would still be smaller than the attack Google faced.

In 2016, a DDoS attack hit a company called Dyn. The attack's botnet had tens of millions of computers.

DDoS attacks may also be political. They can be used as a tool of cyber warfare. Some governments even use DDoS attacks on their own citizens. For example, they may take down news sites. The governments may want to **censor** people who criticize their actions.

19

## CHAPTER 4

# FIGHTING DDoS ATTACKS

People can defend against DDoS attacks in several ways. Groups can take some steps before a DDoS attack happens. For example, they can pay regular attention to their network. That way, they learn what their normal website traffic looks like. Then, a sudden spike from a DDoS attack is easier to spot.

Companies can inform employees about how to look for DDoS attacks.

That helps the organization respond more quickly.

Planning ahead also helps groups respond. Companies often create detailed plans for what to do if a DDoS attack happens. If an attack comes, they don't have to stop and think. They can take their planned steps right away. That can stop DDoS attacks faster.

Groups can prepare their servers, too. Some groups have backup servers. A DDoS attack might take down the main servers. However, the group can switch to the backups. That helps their sites continue functioning. Users may not even notice the cyberattack.

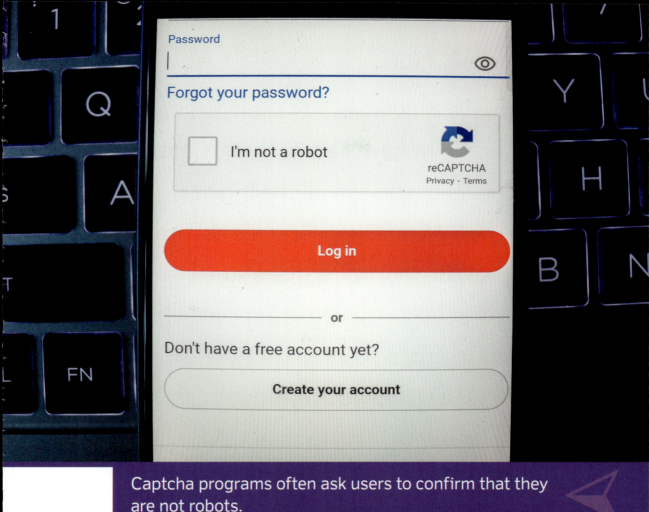

Captcha programs often ask users to confirm that they are not robots.

Some programs help block cyber threats before they happen. Captcha is one example. This program pauses users before entering a site. Users must take an extra step. Captcha often shows

23

users several images. For example, some images might have cars in them. Captcha asks users to click on all the images with cars. After doing so, users can go to the site. The tool helps make sure users are real people. This program can help prevent botnets.

    During a DDoS attack, groups can use a variety of tools to fight back. One method is called IP filtering. All computers that are online get unique markers. They are called IP addresses. Groups can gather this information. They can find out which IP addresses are behind an attack. Then they can block traffic from those addresses.

DDoS attacks are illegal in most countries. Hackers may be convicted and go to prison.

Another tool is called rate limiting. It relates to user activity over a period of time. Groups limit how many requests one user can make. This helps stop botnets from flooding traffic.

Organizations can limit the effects of DDoS attacks in other ways, too. For example, some sites may include fancy features. The sites could be colorful or flashy. These features make the sites more fun to use. But people can still use

## MAFIABOY

In 2000, Michael Calce was just 15 years old. Online, he went by the name Mafiaboy. That year, he carried out a major DDoS attack. The websites of many large companies stopped working. The attack worried US lawmakers. They saw the damage hackers could do. In response, lawmakers passed important cybercrime laws. As an adult, Calce used his talent to help. He began working in cybersecurity.

In 2023, DDoS attacks targeted government websites in Finland. The country worked to strengthen its cybersecurity.

the sites without the features. During DDoS attacks, groups disable the fancy features. That saves data and energy. It helps the server handle traffic during the attack. When the attack is over, the features can be used again.

## CYBER SAFETY

# AVOIDING DDoS ATTACKS

Everyone can help protect against DDoS attacks. First, keeping computers up to date is important. That's because programs often have small problems. Companies use updates to fix problems as they appear. So, users should always install those updates. If they don't, hackers can use the problems for DDoS attacks.

Next, two types of programs can help. Firewalls are one. They stop unsafe traffic coming from the internet. Antivirus software is the other. It finds unsafe things already on the computer. Users should install both types of programs.

People can also keep an eye out for attacks while gaming. A person may get kicked off the game suddenly. Or they may have extreme lag. In those cases, the person should turn off their

Updating programs as soon as possible helps keep computers safe.

console and Wi-Fi. They should unplug the **router**. Then, plug it back in and reset it. That will change the IP address. Hackers will have a harder time accessing the computer.

# FOCUS QUESTIONS

*Write your answers on a separate piece of paper.*

1. Write a paragraph explaining how a distributed denial-of-service (DDoS) attack works.

2. Do you think countries should use cyberattacks during war? Why or why not?

3. What makes a DDoS attack different from a DoS attack?

    **A.** A DDoS attack uses more than one computer.
    **B.** A DDoS attack uses only one computer.
    **C.** A DDoS attack is weaker than a DoS attack.

4. How might a DDoS attack against a company change how people view the company?

    **A.** People might trust the company more.
    **B.** People might believe the company is not safe to use.
    **C.** People might believe the company caused the attack.

*Answer key on page 32.*

# GLOSSARY

**censor**
To stop people from writing or speaking about certain topics.

**consoles**
Computer systems made specifically for video games.

**hackers**
People who illegally gain access to information on computer systems.

**infrastructure**
The systems, such as roads, water supplies, and energy distribution, that a region needs to function.

**lag**
When sounds or images shown by a computer are too slow.

**malware**
Computer programs intended for a bad purpose.

**ransom**
Money paid to stop an attack.

**router**
A device that sends information from one place to another.

**traffic**
The amount of information going around the internet at a certain time.

# TO LEARN MORE

## BOOKS

Bell, Samantha S. *Why Learn Coding?* Abdo Publishing, 2024.

Stratton, Connor. *Great Careers in Technology.* Focus Readers, 2022.

Weakland, Mark. *How Does Wi-Fi Work?* Capstone Press, 2021.

## NOTE TO EDUCATORS

Visit **www.focusreaders.com** to find lesson plans, activities, links, and other resources related to this title.

## INDEX

antivirus software, 28

botnets, 12–13, 24–25

captcha, 23–24
censoring, 19

firewalls, 28

gaming, 16, 28
Google, 18

hackers, 5–7, 11–13, 15–16, 18, 26, 28–29

IP addresses, 24, 29
IP filtering, 24

Mafiaboy, 26
malware, 12

networks, 9–13, 21

ransom, 17

rate limiting, 25
Russia, 5–7

servers, 9–10, 13, 16–18, 22, 27

traffic, 5, 10–11, 13, 16, 18, 21, 24–25, 27, 28

Ukraine, 5–7

Answer Key: 1. Answers will vary; 2. Answers will vary; 3. A; 4. B